# CHILDHOOD TRAUMA

## -The Journey to Healing-

*A Practical Guide to Becoming a Better Person While Healing from Trauma*

## Michelle Brahms

1 |CHILDHOOD TRAUMA

This is not the work of fiction but names, characters, places, and incidents either are the product of the author's imagination or are used fictitiously. Any resemblance to actual persons, living or dead, events, or locales is entirely coincidental

# TABLE OF CONTENT

7 |CHILDHOOD TRAUMA

# INTRODUCTION

## My journey: A Personal Note on Overcoming Trauma

When it comes to trauma, no child truly understands what they're going through or that they'll need to heal from it later in life. In my opinion, this is one of the hardest challenges an adult can face. I know this because I've been there.

I grew up with an emotionally immature parent who struggled to provide me with proper care. I witnessed my parents' divorce and saw them remarry different people. The trauma and pain of not having both parents by my side became a burden I had to carry at the age of 10. Life was tough, and growing up in that environment could have easily turned something beautiful into something bitter. But I fought hard to stay sane, push through, and become a better person - without allowing my experiences to shape me into someone bitter or self-destructive. Over time, I healed.

I'm not here to tell you that healing from trauma is quick or easy - it isn't. My book would be misleading if I suggested otherwise. Healing was a long journey for me, and I traveled it without a guide like the one you're holding. That's why, in this book, I will share everything that helped me stay sane, grow, and eventually heal. Hopefully, by the end of this book, your journey to recovery will be a little shorter than mine - because unlike me, you'll have tools, like a warrior with a weapon.

But before we dive into that, let's take a closer look at what childhood trauma really is.

# Understanding Childhood Trauma: The Deep Impact on Life

Childhood trauma is something that leaves a mark, often in ways we don't even realize until much later. When you're a child, it's hard to make sense of everything that's happening around you. All you know is how it makes you feel - scared, lonely, confused, or even angry. You might not have the words to explain it, but the pain is very real.

Trauma comes in many forms. It can happen because of neglect, abuse, the loss of a loved one, or even growing up in an unstable home where conflict was constant. What's hard to understand when you're young is that this pain doesn't just go away as you grow older. It stays with you and shows up in unexpected ways - through anxiety, fear, difficulty trusting people, or feeling like something is always missing.

The important thing to remember is that none of this is your fault. As children, we don't have the tools or control to stop what's happening around us. But as adults, we can find ways to heal. That's why this book exists - to give you hope, to help you heal, and to show you that there's a path forward, no matter how tough your past may have been.

# The Path Forward: Healing Without Losing Your Humanity

Healing from childhood trauma isn't easy, and it's not quick. But it's possible. The road might be long, but with time and patience, you can find peace again. You might worry that you'll always carry this burden, that it will change who you are or make it impossible for you to live a happy, fulfilling life. But here's the truth: **You don't have to let your trauma define you.**

You can heal and still be the kind, loving, and strong person you want to be. In fact, going through this process of healing can bring out an even deeper sense of compassion - for yourself and for others. You learn how to be gentle with your own pain, and in doing so, you become someone who understands and cares for others in a way that's truly special.

Healing doesn't mean you forget or erase the past. It means you learn to live with it in a way that doesn't hold you back or make you bitter. It's about finding a way to carry those experiences without letting them control your life. Yes, it's hard. Yes, it takes time. But little by little, you can heal. And when you do, you'll discover that your experiences, as painful as they were, don't have to rob you of your joy, your love, or your humanity.

This book is here to help you with that. You are not alone, and there is hope for healing - even if it feels far away right now. Together, we will walk through this journey, one step at a time, toward a life where you are no longer defined by what happened to you, but by the strength, kindness, and courage that lives within you.

# PART 1

# Acknowledging the Past Without Letting It Define You

# CHAPTER 1

## Recognizing Childhood Trauma

### What Childhood Trauma Looks Like

Many people think trauma has to be something extreme to count, but that's not true. Childhood trauma can be anything that caused deep emotional pain when you were young. It could be things like feeling unloved, being left out, or not having your needs met. It could also be bigger events like losing a parent, witnessing violence, or growing up in a home where there was a lot of arguing or tension.

The thing about trauma is that it leaves invisible scars. You might not see them, but they affect the way you feel, think, and behave as you grow older. It's important to understand what trauma looks like so you can start recognizing how it may still be affecting you today.

"The feeling of trauma is your body reminding you that something is went wrong inside and they have been trying to heal you"

## Emotional and Behavioral Consequences

When we carry trauma from childhood, it can show up in many ways. You might find it hard to trust people, or maybe you always feel like something is wrong even when things are okay. You might experience anxiety, depression, or even moments of intense anger that seem to come out of nowhere.

The good news is, once you know where these feelings come from, you can start working on them. You don't have to live with them forever. This book will help you understand those feelings and begin the process of healing.

## Why Trauma Doesn't Have to Control You

Your trauma may be part of your story, but it doesn't have to control your life. Yes, it has shaped some parts of who you are, but it doesn't define everything about you. You are still capable of love, happiness, and growth. Recognizing trauma is the first step toward taking back control of your life.

# CHAPTER 2

## Separating Your Worth from Your Wounds

**Understanding Self-Worth Beyond Pain**

One of the hardest things about trauma is that it can make you feel like you're not good enough. Maybe you grew up feeling like you weren't loved or valued, and that feeling sticks with you even now. But here's the truth: **Your worth is not based on what happened to you.** You are valuable, and you deserve love and kindness - especially from yourself.

Healing begins with learning to see yourself as more than your pain. You are not defined by what you went through. You are so much more than that.

16 |CHILDHOOD TRAUMA

## Reframing the Narrative: You Are More Than Your Trauma

It's easy to get caught in the story of your trauma, where everything feels connected to what happened in the past. But there's another way to look at things. Instead of seeing yourself as broken, start seeing yourself as strong for surviving. You've been through hard things, but that doesn't mean you're damaged. It means you're resilient.

Changing the way, you think about your story is a powerful step in healing. You are not a victim of your past - you are a survivor with the ability to write a new chapter in your life.

## Building Emotional Resilience

Emotional resilience is what helps you bounce back from life's challenges. It's the ability to feel pain but not let it break you. And the good news is, you can build resilience with time and practice. Start by being gentle with yourself. When difficult emotions come up, don't push them away. Acknowledge them, feel them, and then let them go.

Resilience doesn't mean ignoring your pain - it means facing it with courage and knowing you can get through it.

# CHAPTER 3

# The Importance of Facing Your Trauma

## How Avoidance Hinders Healing

I'll admit, during my healing journey, I often distracted myself—whether by shifting my thoughts, having random conversations, or even singing a song—just to avoid slipping into the painful memories It's tempting to avoid thinking about the things that hurt us. But avoidance doesn't make the pain go away - it just pushes it down, where it can still affect us in ways we don't always see. When we avoid our trauma, it can show up as anxiety, anger, or feelings of being stuck in life.

Facing your trauma might feel scary, but it's a necessary step to healing. It doesn't mean you have to relive every painful memory. It just means being honest with yourself about how the past still affects you today.

## Safe Ways to Confront Difficult Memories

You don't have to do this all at once, and you definitely don't have to do it alone. Start small. Maybe it's talking to a trusted friend, writing down your feelings, or seeing a therapist who can guide you through the process. The key is to approach your trauma gently, without rushing.

Remember, healing isn't about diving into the deep end. It's about taking small, manageable steps toward feeling better.

## The Role of Therapy and Self-Reflection

Though I wrote this book as a guide for you, I believe that you need more than this piece to go through this journey – you need a listening ear, and one of the things that helped me was talking to someone, yes, because, sometimes, we need help from someone who understands trauma and knows how to guide us through it. Therapy can be a safe space to explore your feelings and find ways to heal. There are many types of therapy, so finding one that feels right for you is important.

Self-reflection is also a powerful tool. Taking time to think about your emotions, your reactions, and what triggers your pain can give you valuable insights into yourself. Healing starts with understanding, and both therapy and self-reflection can help you get there.

**End of Part 1**

In Part 1, we've taken the first steps in understanding what trauma is, how it affects us, and why facing it is important for healing. My aim is that you recognize that your worth goes far beyond the painful things you've been through. Remember, this is a journey, and each step you take brings you closer to the peace and strength you deserve.

# PART 2

## Cultivating a Positive Lifestyle Amidst Trauma Recovery

Healing from trauma is not just about working through the pain - it's also about finding ways to live positively and take care of yourself, even while you're still healing. It's easy to feel overwhelmed by everything that's happened, but life doesn't stop, and neither do the small moments that bring joy and hope. In this part of the book, we'll explore practical ways to build a life that feels good, even when healing is still a work in progress.

# CHAPTER 4

# Embracing Positivity in a Chaotic World

Life can be tough, especially when you've been through trauma. It's easy to feel like the world is against you or that nothing ever goes right. But one of the most powerful tools you have is your mindset. Choosing to look for the good, even when things are hard, can make a huge difference.

## The Power of Optimism in Overcoming Hardships

Optimism doesn't mean pretending everything is perfect - it just means believing that good things can still happen, even in the middle of difficult times. It's about holding on to hope, even when it's just a small flicker. When you train your mind to see the positive, it helps you push through the tough moments and keeps you moving forward.

## Practicing Gratitude Daily

One simple way to stay positive is by practicing gratitude. This doesn't mean ignoring the pain you're feeling; it just means taking a few moments each day to notice the little things that are going right. Maybe it's a kind word from a friend, the warmth of the sun on your face, or simply having a moment of peace. These small things remind you that there is still good in the world - and in your life.

## Shifting Perspectives: Finding Meaning in Small Victories

Healing is a long journey, but along the way, there are small victories. Maybe you handled a tough conversation better than you thought you would, or you got through a day without feeling overwhelmed by your past. These moments matter. Celebrate them, no matter how small they seem, because they are steps toward a better life.

# CHAPTER 5

## The Good Person Within

Sometimes, when you've been hurt, it's easy to think that the world doesn't deserve your kindness. But deep down, you know that being a good person - despite what you've been through - makes you stronger, not weaker. I suppose my trauma ultimately helped me in an unexpected way—it made me determined not to become the very monster I despised. I refused to be the person who abandons others without reason or leaves them during their most vulnerable moments. Instead, I became the opposite of what my trauma was trying to turn me into. Your trauma doesn't have to define how you treat others or yourself.

## Why Trauma Doesn't Justify Toxic Behavior

It's tempting to lash out when you're hurting. Maybe you've been treated badly, and part of you wants to give that pain right back to the world. But here's the thing: carrying your trauma into your relationships or behavior only makes the hurt grow. You don't have to let what happened to you make you into someone you don't want to be. Choosing kindness, even when it's hard, is part of the healing process.

## Acting with Integrity in All Circumstances

Acting with integrity means doing what's right, even when no one is watching. It's easy to let pain cloud your judgment, but staying true to your values helps you heal. Every time you choose honesty, compassion, or fairness, you're reinforcing the fact that your trauma doesn't control you - you control your choices.

## Compassion as a Healing Tool for Yourself and Others

Being compassionate isn't just about being kind to others - it's about being kind to yourself, too. When you offer yourself the same understanding and forgiveness you give to others, you open up space for healing. Trauma often leaves us feeling unworthy, but practicing compassion toward yourself helps remind you that you deserve love and care just as much as anyone else.

# CHAPTER 6

## Building Healthy Habits for Emotional Strength

Healing isn't just about dealing with the past; it's also about creating habits that support your mental and emotional health. Taking care of yourself is one of the most important things you can do during your healing journey.

## Practical Ways to Cultivate Emotional Stability

Creating emotional stability doesn't happen overnight, but there are simple, practical things you can do each day to help. This might mean journaling about your feelings, talking to a trusted friend, or even just taking a few deep breaths when you feel overwhelmed. Little by little, these habits build emotional strength.

## The Role of Physical Health in Mental Recovery

It's easy to forget how closely our physical health is tied to our mental well-being. When we take care of our bodies—by eating well, getting enough sleep, and staying active - it helps our minds heal, too. Something as simple as a walk outside or a few stretches in the morning can do wonders for your mood and mental clarity.

## Mindfulness and Meditation Techniques for Healing

Mindfulness and meditation are powerful tools for staying grounded. Mindfulness helps you stay present, which is especially helpful when memories from the past feel overwhelming. Meditation, even just for a few minutes a day, can help calm your mind and give you the space to process your emotions without being consumed by them.

# PART 2



# Conclusion: A Path Forward

Healing from trauma doesn't mean everything suddenly becomes easy. But by making small changes, embracing positive habits, and remembering your own goodness, you can build a life that feels lighter and brighter, even in the midst of recovery. It's about taking one step at a time—celebrating each moment of progress and being gentle with yourself when things feel hard.

# PART 3

## Healing Without Hurting Others or Yourself

When we go through deep pain, it can sometimes feel like that pain spills over into other parts of our lives. We might hurt the people around us without even meaning to, or we might hurt ourselves through negative habits. The truth is, healing doesn't just mean overcoming the past - it also means learning how to break those harmful cycles and treat yourself and others with love and care. In this part, we'll explore how to heal while staying kind, both to yourself and those around you.

# CHAPTER 7

## Breaking Negative Cycles

Healing from trauma can feel like breaking free from a cycle. You might notice that certain patterns keep showing up in your life – personally my first boyfriend abandon me, my best friend did the same, my boss retrench me from office, and I ended a good relationship that didn't cause me any pains simply because I didn't want to give my opponent the power to break me again. Yours may be the opposite whether it's pushing people away, sabotaging good opportunities, or feeling like you're not worthy of love and happiness. These cycles are tough to break, but recognizing them is the first step.

Start by being honest with yourself about the ways you might be holding yourself back. It's okay to admit that sometimes we stand in our own way - it's part of being human. The key is to approach these moments with gentleness. Don't blame yourself. Instead, ask yourself, "What can I learn from this?" With that mindset, you can start to shift those patterns and create healthier habits.

Remember, breaking these cycles doesn't happen overnight. It's about taking small steps. Forgive yourself when you slip up, and celebrate every little victory along the way. Every time you choose a better path, you're getting closer to the person you want to become.

# CHAPTER 8

## Setting Boundaries While Healing

Setting boundaries can be one of the most powerful tools in your healing process. Well, I won't lie on this one, it was a really big struggle for me because when you've experienced trauma, it's easy to feel like your needs don't matter, or that saying "no" will upset people. But here's the thing: **You have a right to protect your peace**

Sometimes, I found myself pushing people away, craving isolation, even though deep down, I needed them the most. The fear of being abandoned again, of reliving the pain and memories, was too much to bear. I convinced myself that keeping people at a distance was a kind of boundary, like a way of protecting myself. I thought, "If I don't let anything start, there's nothing to heal from." You know, like the saying, "If you don't want to taste the pain, don't take a bite." It felt safer to avoid the hurt altogether because, after all, no one willingly walks into something they already know will hurt.

But is true that setting boundaries is not about pushing people away or being harsh. It's about recognizing your own limits and knowing what's healthy for you. It might be as simple as saying no to situations that stress you out, or taking time for yourself when you need it. It's okay to step back from relationships or environments that make your healing harder.

The tricky part is doing this without feeling guilty. But remember, boundaries are not selfish—they are necessary. When you set clear boundaries, you protect your emotional space and allow yourself to heal without being overwhelmed by others' demands. And when you're in a better place, you'll have more to give to those you care about, without feeling drained.

# CHAPTER 9

## The Importance of Emotional Honesty

'It wasn't really that bad? I'm not hurt I think I have been overstressed lately and need to sleep' many times I had fed myself this lie just to see ways to escape the sting and probably feel better but it never goes away. Yours may be different but I want you to know that emotional honesty is a big part of healing. It's about being real with yourself about what you're feeling, instead of bottling it up or pretending you're fine when you're not. It's okay to feel hurt, sad, or even angry about what happened. Pushing those emotions away doesn't make them disappear - it just delays the healing.

Talking about your feelings can be incredibly freeing. You don't have to share everything with everyone, but having someone you trust - whether it's a friend, family member, or therapist - can make a huge difference. Sometimes just saying the words out loud helps release the weight of what you've been carrying inside.

But emotional honesty isn't just about sharing with others. It's also about being honest with yourself. Acknowledge your pain, but also recognize the progress you're making. Be proud of how far you've come, even if the journey feels slow. And remember, being honest with your emotions doesn't make you weak - it makes you strong.

Healing without hurting others or yourself means taking responsibility for your actions while being kind to yourself. I can say this with boldness that I did great on this aspect because I got to understand that it means learning to forgive, not just those who hurt you, but also yourself for any mistakes you may have made along the way. In this part of the book, we've focused on practical steps like breaking negative cycles, setting boundaries, and practicing emotional honesty - all of which are important in becoming the best version of yourself while you heal.

Healing is a journey, not a straight line. You'll have good days and tough days, but each step you take brings you closer to the peace and happiness you deserve. Be patient with yourself, and remember: you are worthy of healing.

I hope this aligns with your vision! It's designed to be warm, practical, and easy to understand. Let me know your thoughts!

# PART 4

## Achieving Gradual and Sustainable Healing

# CHAPTER 10

# Reclaiming Your Future from Trauma

## Envisioning a Future Not Defined by the Past

It's easy to feel like your trauma will always control your future, but it doesn't have to be that way. Many times, I had broken down in fear that i may never find healing in the future, the thought of it make daily life miserable and I really won't want someone going through trauma to feel that way because you can achieve happiness. Healing means starting to believe in a future that's filled with possibilities, not pain. Take a moment to imagine what life could look like when you're not held back by the weight of the past. It doesn't mean everything will be perfect, but it means you'll be free to live, love, and dream again. This is your chance to take back control and rewrite your future, step by step.

## Personal Growth and Rediscovery

As you heal, you'll start rediscovering parts of yourself that may have been hidden or pushed aside because of your trauma. Maybe there's something you loved as a child, like drawing, writing, or just being outside, but you haven't done it in years. Now is the time to reconnect with those parts of yourself. Healing is not just about fixing what's broken—it's also about finding what's still beautiful inside you and allowing it to flourish.

## What Healing Looks Like: Small Milestones to Celebrate

If anyone ever told you stuff like 'You've outgrown childhood you shouldn't look at it anyone' they may be discouraging you from being patient and allowing yourself follow the pattern of healing. After all who says it happens overnight. Sometimes though you may find yourself in that ditch of wanting to heal immediately and may end up being unkind and understanding to yourself. Healing doesn't happen overnight. It's a journey with small steps that deserve to be celebrated. Maybe today you were able to get through the day without feeling overwhelmed. Maybe you opened up to someone you trust. These moments, no matter how small they seem, are victories. Give yourself credit for every bit of progress. Healing is made up of these small, quiet milestones, and they all matter.

# CHAPTER 11

## Healing Is a journey, not a Destination

### The Myth of Complete Healing

There's an idea out there that once you heal, you'll never have to deal with your trauma again. But that's not always how it works because even till this moment, during my time of self-reflect, the thought of abandonment hit me so hard sometimes and the pains seems to return in a blink, so healing is more of a journey than a destination. There will be days when you feel completely free from your past, everything seems fine, and then there might be days when it sneaks back in, and that's okay. It doesn't mean you haven't healed - it just means you're human. The goal isn't to be perfect remember?! but to keep moving forward, even on the tough days.

# Managing Relapses and Setbacks

Setbacks are part of the process, and they don't erase the progress you've made. When you hit a rough patch, it's easy to feel like you're back at square one, but you're not. Think of it like climbing a hill. Sometimes you might slip, but that doesn't mean you haven't already climbed higher than before. When setbacks happen, be gentle with yourself. It's just a bump in the road, not the end of the journey.

## Staying on the Healing Path with Patience and Self-Compassion

Patience is key in this journey. Healing takes time, and it's important to be kind to yourself along the way. Self-compassion means treating yourself like you would treat a dear friend—without harsh judgment, and with plenty of understanding. When you're tired or feeling down, remind yourself that it's okay to rest. Healing isn't a race, and there's no right or wrong way to do it. Just take it one day at a time.

# CHAPTER 12

## Finding Your Purpose Beyond Trauma

### Channeling Pain into Personal Purpose

One of the most powerful ways to heal is to take the pain you've experienced and turn it into something meaningful. Maybe you can use your story to help others, or maybe your journey leads you to find a new passion or purpose. The pain you've been through doesn't have to just be a burden - it can also be a source of strength and inspiration. Finding purpose beyond trauma can give you a new sense of direction and help you feel more in control of your life.

## Helping Others While Healing Yourself

As you heal, you may find that you have the ability to help others who are going through similar struggles. This doesn't mean you have to be fully healed before you can help - sometimes, just sharing your story or offering a listening ear can make a big difference for someone else. Helping others can also reinforce your own healing, reminding you that you're not alone in this journey.

## How Your Experience Can Empower Others

Your story is powerful, and it has the potential to empower not only yourself but also others. By sharing your journey and the lessons you've learned, you can give others hope that healing is possible. You don't have to have all the answers or be completely healed to inspire someone else. Just by being open and honest, you can help others see that they too can overcome their trauma and build a better future

# CONCLUSION

Let's take a moment to reflect on everything we've explored together.

## PART 1

## Acknowledging the Past Without Letting It Define You

We began by recognizing what childhood trauma looks like. It's often hard to identify at first, but once we understand its impact, we can start to separate who we are from what happened to us. Remember, your trauma is not your fault, and it doesn't define your worth. Facing it is hard, but it's the first step toward healing.

We also talked about the importance of self-worth. You are more than your wounds, and you deserve to live a life free from the weight of your past. Building emotional resilience and learning to stand tall in the face of your trauma takes time, but it's possible.

# PART 2

## Cultivating a Positive Lifestyle Amidst Trauma Recovery

Next, we explored how to live a positive life even while healing. It's not about pretending everything is fine but about finding hope in the little things. Gratitude, optimism, and small victories are powerful tools in your healing process.

We also talked about the importance of being a good person, even when life hasn't been kind to you. Trauma can make us feel angry or bitter, but you've chosen to rise above that. By acting with integrity and compassion, both toward yourself and others, you're already on the path to becoming the best version of yourself.

And don't forget the healthy habits we discussed. Emotional stability, physical health, and mindfulness all work together to help you stay grounded. These small daily practices can make a huge difference in how you feel over time.

# PART 3

# Healing Without Hurting Others or Yourself

In this section, we talked about breaking the negative cycles that trauma often creates. It's easy to fall into patterns of self-sabotage or to project your pain onto others, but recognizing these habits is the first step to changing them. Remember, you have the power to stop those cycles and create new, healthier ones.

We also discussed setting boundaries. Healing doesn't mean you have to keep everyone happy. It means protecting your peace and knowing when to say 'no.' Boundaries aren't selfish, they're necessary for your well-being.

And finally, we talked about the importance of emotional honesty. It's okay to be real about your pain. You don't have to hide how you're feeling, and it's okay to ask for support from those you trust. Sharing your journey with others can help lighten the load.

# PART 4

## Achieving Gradual and Sustainable Healing

As we moved into the final part of the book, we talked about reclaiming your future. Trauma may have shaped parts of your past, but it doesn't get to write the story of your future. You are in control of what comes next. Healing is a process, and it doesn't happen overnight, but with patience, you can create the life you want.

We also touched on the idea that healing is not a destination. There's no magic moment when everything suddenly feels perfect. There will be setbacks, but that's okay. What matters is that you keep moving forward, even if some days are harder than others.

Lastly, we discussed finding your purpose beyond trauma. Your experiences have given you strength and insight, and now, you can use that to help others. Whether that means simply being kind to someone who's struggling or sharing your story, your journey has the potential to inspire and uplift others.

My sincere words to you

Before we part, I want to say this: You are so much stronger than you know. Healing isn't easy, I wasn't easy for me too, I did and now you've already come so far. You've taken the brave step of facing your past, learning about yourself, and working toward a better future. And that's something to be incredibly proud of.

This book was never meant to be a quick fix, because healing takes time. But I hope it has been a helpful companion on your journey. I hope it has given you tools, insights, and, most importantly - hope.

As you move forward, be kind to yourself, I also struggle with this while on my journey to heal, I was trying to get the healing done quickly and therefore will bet myself up for set-backs. But as time goes on I learnt to celebrate the little effort that my really not be enough, so celebrate your progress, no matter how small it may seem. Surround yourself with love and support, and remember that you're not alone on this journey.

You are capable of healing. You are deserving of peace. And you are worthy of a life filled with joy, purpose, and love.

Thank you for letting me be part of your healing journey.